THE DISTANCE SITUATION

Love Unbound by Miles

RAMAKRISHNAN

notionpress.com
INDIA · SINGAPORE · MALAYSIA

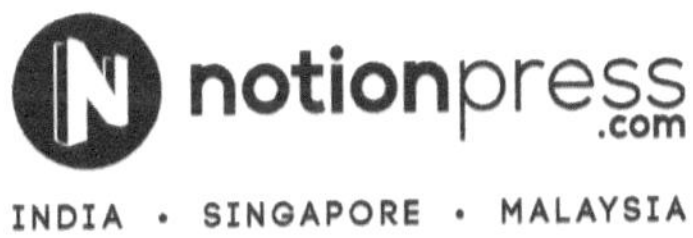

ISBN
Paperback 979-8-89556-992-4
Hardcase 979-8-89673-810-7

Contents

Chapter 1

Introduction to Long-Distance Love

Why Do Most Regular Relationships End in Breakups?

Relationships, whether they are close proximity or long-distance, can end for various reasons. Breakups in geographically close relationships, often referred to as 'regular' relationships, can typically be traced back to several key factors:

Certainly! Here's a simplified explanation of each reason why relationships might end, accompanied by relevant quotes:

1. Communication Issues: When partners don't communicate effectively, misunderstandings can occur, and problems go unresolved.

"The single biggest problem in communication is the illusion that it has taken place."

— George Bernard Shaw.

---

2. Incompatibility: Sometimes, partners might find they want different things in life or have different values, which can make it hard to stay together.

"Sometimes good things fall apart so better things can fall together."

— Marilyn Monroe.

---

3. Loss of Connection or Interest: If partners stop paying attention to each other and don't maintain their emotional or physical connection, they may start to feel distant.

*"Indifference and neglect often
do much more damage than
outright dislike."*

— *J.K. Rowling.*

4. Trust Issues: Trust is crucial in a relationship. If it's broken through dishonesty or infidelity, it can be very hard to repair.

*"Trust takes years to build,
seconds to break, and forever
to repair."*

— *Unknown.*

5. Life Changes and Personal Growth: As individuals grow and their lives change, their relationships might not fit their new circumstances or selves.

*"We are products of our
past, but we don't have to be
prisoners of it."*

— *Rick Warren.*

6. Financial Stress: Money problems can lead to stress and fights if partners disagree on spending or face financial hardship.

> **"When money becomes an issue, love becomes an account."**
>
> — *Raheel Farooq.*

7. Unmet Expectations: If a relationship doesn't meet the expectations one or both partners had, it can lead to disappointment and heartache.

> ***Expectation is the root of all heartache."***
>
> — *William Shakespeare.*

8. Lack of Effort: A relationship needs both partners to actively work on it. If one or both stop trying, the relationship can weaken and eventually end.

> *"Any relationship is like a priority list. If it's not at the top of that list, it might be time to cross it off altogether."*
>
> — *Unknown.*

9. Conflict and Arguments: Disagreements are normal, but constant or unresolved conflict can harm the relationship.

> *"Peace is not the absence of conflict, it is the ability to handle conflict by peaceful means."*
>
> — *Ronald Reagan.*

10. External Influences: Pressure from family, friends, or cultural expectations can impact how partners see their relationship and each other.

> *"Let no one who loves be unhappy, even love unreturned has its rainbow."*
>
> — *James M. Barrie.*

Adding to the reasons relationships might face challenges or end, two important aspects to consider are disrespect for personal freedom and invasion of personal space. Here's how these issues can impact relationships:

11. Disrespect for Personal Freedom: When one partner tries to control or limit the other's choices, it can lead to feelings of suffocation and resentment. This disrespect for personal freedom might manifest as one partner dictating who the other can see, what they can do, or even what they can wear.

"The greatest gifts you can give your children are the roots of responsibility and the wings of independence."

— *Denis Waitley.*

This quote, although often applied to parenting, is also relevant to romantic relationships, where both partners should feel free to be themselves and make their own choices.

12. Invasion of Personal Space: Everyone needs a certain amount of privacy, even from their partner. When one partner doesn't respect these boundaries, it can lead to tension and discomfort. This might include

reading messages without permission, insisting on being together all the time, or not allowing any private time.

"Privacy is not something that I'm merely entitled to, it's an absolute prerequisite."

— *Marlon Brando.*

This quote emphasises the importance of maintaining individual privacy, which is essential for a healthy and balanced relationship.

Addressing these issues involves open communication about boundaries, a mutual understanding of independence within the relationship, and respect for each partner's need for personal space and freedom. Failing to do so can undermine the relationship's foundation, potentially leading to its end.

Understanding the Dynamics of Long-Distance Relationships (LDRs)

Understanding the dynamics of long-distance relationships involves recognising their unique challenges and opportunities. Here are some key aspects to consider:

1. Emotional Connection

   - Intensity and Depth: Relationships at a distance often exhibit greater emotional intensity as partners engage in deeper communication to compensate for the lack of physical presence.

   - Appreciation of Time Together: The time spent together in long-distance relationships is usually less frequent but highly cherished, often leading to more meaningful interactions.

2. Communication

   - Frequency and Modes: Effective long-distance relationships depend on regular communication via texts, calls, video chats, and social media.

   - Quality Over Quantity: Focusing on meaningful conversations rather than the sheer number of messages can deepen the relationship.

3. Trust and Security

   - Building Trust: Trust is especially crucial in LDRs, where partners can't see each other's daily lives. It must be built through consistent, honest actions over time.

   - Handling Insecurities: The physical distance can exacerbate insecurities. Openly addressing these feelings and providing mutual reassurances is vital.

4. Independence and Interdependence

    - Balancing Lives: Maintaining a balance between independence and the relationship is essential for personal health and relationship vitality.

    - Support Systems: Strong external support systems are crucial for personal fulfilment and can enhance the relationship's health.

5. Planning and Future Goals

    - Short-Term Plans: Regularly planning visits and special occasions keeps the relationship dynamic and forward-looking.

    - Long-Term Outlook: Discussing and aligning on future goals, including plans to eventually live in the same location, is key.

6. Adaptability and Resilience

    - Dealing with Change: Adaptability is crucial in managing life's changes, from schedule shifts to emotional developments.

    - Resilience: The inherent challenges of LDRs require strong resilience and commitment from both partners.

7. Cultural and Social Considerations

    - Different Backgrounds: Partners from different backgrounds can use the distance as an opportunity to explore and appreciate diverse perspectives.

- Social Perceptions: It's important to manage societal views and external opinions on the viability of LDRs.

8. Personal Interests

   - Maintaining Individuality: Continuing personal hobbies and interests helps maintain a strong sense of self and provides fresh content to share in conversations.

   - Shared Interests: Developing shared activities that can be done together remotely, such as online classes or gaming, helps strengthen the bond.

9. Conflict Resolution in Long-Distance Relationships

Handling Disagreements: Learning effective strategies for resolving conflicts from a distance is crucial. Traditional calming gestures, such as touch, are not an option, making verbal and emotional reassurances paramount. It's important to quickly address misunderstandings and to always consider the impact of words before speaking.

Preventive Measures: Establishing clear communication guidelines and regularly discussing potential stress points are essential to prevent misunderstandings. It's beneficial to never let disputes linger beyond a few minutes. Always consider the importance of the relationship over the disagreement. Before escalating any issue, take a moment to decide whether the issue at hand is more critical than your relationship. Remember, everyone makes mistakes, and often, it's best to address the issue calmly or choose to let it go for the sake of harmony.

By incorporating these approaches, couples can manage disagreements more effectively, maintaining a stronger, more understanding relationship despite the physical distance.

10. Role of Technology

- Technological Tools: Utilising the full spectrum of available technologies, from messaging apps to virtual reality, can help bridge the physical gap.

- Innovative Interaction: Creative use of technology, such as watching movies together online or virtual reality dates, can simulate shared experiences.

By understanding these dynamics, individuals and couples can not only navigate, but also flourish in long-distance relationships, transforming challenges into opportunities for growth and deeper connections.

Debunking Myths and Misconceptions About Long-Distance Relationships

Long-distance relationships (LDRs) are often surrounded by scepticism and myths that can discourage couples from pursuing or maintaining them. However, understanding and debunking these misconceptions is crucial for fostering a healthy, enduring connection despite the miles.

Myth 1: Long-Distance Relationships Are Bound to Fail.

A common belief is that all long-distance relationships are doomed from the start. However, research and anecdotal evidence suggest that LDRs have about the same success rates as geographically close relationships. The critical factors influencing their success include the level of commitment, communication, and a shared vision for the future. Technology has also made it easier for couples to stay connected, diminishing the physical distance with video calls, instant messaging, and social media.

Myth 2: LDRs Lack Emotional Intimacy

Many assume that physical separation leads to emotional distance. On the contrary, couples in long-distance relationships often experience increased intimacy because they engage in deeper and more frequent communication to compensate for the lack of physical presence. These couples may end up knowing each other better due to their emphasis on communication and sharing.

Myth 3: High Levels of Jealousy and Insecurity Are Inevitable.

While jealousy and insecurity can occur in any relationship, they are not specific to or more prevalent in LDRs. Success in long-distance relationships hinges on trust and open communication. Couples who openly discuss their fears, expectations, and daily experiences tend to develop a robust trust that mitigates insecurities and jealous tendencies.

Myth 4: Long-Distance Is Easier Than Close Proximity Relationships

This myth stems from the notion that LDRs require less daily effort. In reality, maintaining affection and connection over a distance demands significant commitment and creativity. Planning visits, aligning schedules across time zones, and ensuring quality communication are ongoing efforts that require time and energy.

Myth 5: Long-Distance Is Merely a Temporary Arrangement

While some view LDRs as a short-term solution until couples can reunite, many see it as a foundational stage of a lifelong partnership. These relationships can be just as committed and serious as those of couples who live together. Often, the distance is a stepping stone to a more permanent future together.

Understanding these truths helps those in long-distance relationships overcome challenges, debunk myths and build stronger, more resilient partnerships.

Chapter 2

The Art of Communication

How Do You Find the Right Person

Finding the right romantic partner involves self-awareness, clear communication, and understanding what you truly seek in a relationship. Here are key steps to help you identify a compatible partner:

1. Know Yourself: Start by understanding your own desires, values, and goals. This self-awareness will guide you in finding someone who shares similar aspirations and values, which are crucial for long-term compatibility.

2. Expand Your Social Circle: Increase your chances of meeting potential partners by engaging in social activities that reflect your interests. Whether it's through sports clubs, cultural events, or online

forums, expanding your network can lead you to like-minded individuals.

3. Prioritise Communication: Effective communication is essential. Look for someone who expresses themselves clearly and listens actively. This skill is vital for resolving conflicts and building a strong foundation in a relationship.

4. Observe Actions: Actions often speak louder than words. Pay attention to how potential partners treat others and themselves. Consistent, respectful behaviour is a good indicator of character and how they will treat you in a relationship.

5. Take Your Time: Don't rush into a relationship. Taking time to get to know someone helps in understanding their true nature and your compatibility with them.

6. Look for Mutual Respect and Support: Choose a partner who respects your boundaries and supports your personal and professional growth. Mutual respect and encouragement are the backbone of any healthy relationship.

7. Elevate Each Other: Find someone who not only aligns with you but also inspires and encourages your personal growth. A good partner should enhance your life, helping both of you to become better individuals and a stronger couple.

8. Trust Your Instincts: Sometimes, despite a perfect-seeming alignment on paper, your instincts might signal a mismatch. Trust these feelings. Feeling at ease and valued are signs of a promising relationship.

9. Be Patient and Realistic: Finding the right person for an LDR doesn't happen overnight. Be patient with the process and maintain realistic expectations about what the relationship can offer and the extra effort it will require.

In sum, the right partner is someone who complements your life and with whom you can share a mutually uplifting future. This relationship should not only meet your desires but also enhance your personal and collective growth.

How to Start a Relationship?

Starting a relationship can be an exciting and enriching experience, requiring thoughtful consideration and proactive engagement. Here's a guide to help you embark on this new journey in a healthy and fulfilling way:

1. Establishing a Strong Friendship: Foundation is key in any relationship. Begin by building a strong friendship where you both feel comfortable sharing your thoughts, interests, and feelings. This establishes trust and deepens your understanding of

each other, providing a solid base for a romantic relationship.

2. Communicate Openly and Honestly: Effective communication is crucial. Express your feelings, desires, and expectations early on. Be clear about what you're looking for in a relationship and ensure that your values and life goals align. Open dialogue fosters transparency and reduces misunderstandings.

3. Spend Quality Time Together: Spending time together helps you learn more about each other's habits, behaviours, and reactions to different situations. Whether it's going out on dates, engaging in mutual hobbies, or simply having quiet evenings at home, quality time strengthens your connection.

4. Show Respect and Appreciation: Respect each other's opinions, feelings, and boundaries. Showing appreciation for the little things your partner does can go a long way in building mutual respect and admiration, which are essential for a healthy relationship.

5. Be Patient and Take It Slow: Allow the relationship to develop naturally at its own pace. Rushing into deeper commitment can create unnecessary pressure. It's important to enjoy the journey of getting to know each other without rushing through relationship milestones.

6. Meet Each Other's Social Circle: Introducing each other to friends and family is a step towards integrating your lives. Seeing how your partner interacts with your social circle can also provide deeper insights into their personality and values.

7. Address Conflicts Constructively: No relationship is without conflicts. When disagreements arise, address them constructively. Avoid blame and focus on how you can solve the issue together. Effective problem-solving strengthens relationships by building trust and understanding.

8. Maintain Independence: While it's important to grow together, maintaining your independence, including your personal hobbies and social life, is essential. This balance ensures a healthy dynamic where both individuals can grow individually and as a couple.

Starting a relationship with these mindful strategies will help ensure that your new connection is not only joyful, but also has the potential for long-term success.

Tip #1: Never hold any fights for more than 5 minutes.

Mastering Various Communication Tools and Platforms

Mastering various communication tools and platforms is crucial in today's digitally connected world, especially for maintaining personal and professional relationships across distances. Whether you're navigating a long-distance relationship, working remotely, or keeping in touch with friends and family, effective use of communication technologies can enhance your interactions and ensure you stay connected. Here are some key considerations for mastering these tools:

1. Choose the Right Tools: Start by selecting the appropriate communication platforms based on your needs. For personal interactions, instant messaging apps like WhatsApp or social media platforms like Facebook can be ideal for casual, frequent updates. Video conferencing apps like Zoom, Google Meet, or WhatsApp are essential for more direct and personal interaction, allowing for nuances like facial expressions and body language.

2. Understand the Features: Each platform has unique features designed to enhance communication. Take the time to learn these features. For instance, understanding how to share screens on Skype or use channels on Slack can improve your communication efficiency and effectiveness.

3. Maintain Etiquette: Digital communication has its own set of etiquettes. Be mindful of response times, appropriate messaging hours, and the tone of your messages. For professional communications, maintaining a formal tone is usually appropriate, whereas personal chats might allow for more casual interaction.

4. Regular Updates: Especially in a long-distance relationship or a remote working arrangement, regular updates can help reduce feelings of disconnect. Share updates about your day, discuss plans, or even send a photo of something interesting you encountered. These small gestures can make a big difference in maintaining a sense of closeness.

5. Secure Your Communications: With the increasing use of digital platforms, securing your online communications is crucial. Use strong, unique passwords for different platforms, and enable two-factor authentication where available to protect your information from unauthorised access.

6. Adapt to Your Audience: Tailor your communication style to suit the person you are interacting with. Some may prefer brief and direct messages, while others might appreciate more detailed and frequent updates. Adjusting your communication approach can lead to more effective interactions and stronger relationships.

By mastering various communication tools and platforms, you not only enhance your ability to stay connected, but also ensure that every interaction is meaningful and productive. Whether for personal bonds or professional teamwork, effective communication is a key component of success in our interconnected world.

TIPS#2 Always consider whether you value the person or the argument before attempting to resolve the issue, or decide to let it go, as mistakes can happen.

Effective Communication Strategies to Maintain Emotional Closeness

Maintaining emotional closeness in any relationship, especially in a long-distance one, hinges crucially on effective communication strategies. Here are some approaches that can help partners stay emotionally connected despite physical separation:

1. Prioritise Regular Communication: Consistency is key to keeping the emotional connection alive. "We are wired to connect with others literally every second of the day," states Dr. Amir Levine. This is why regular check-ins and updates, even about mundane aspects of daily life, can make each person feel included and valued in the other's life.

2. Utilise Various Communication Tools: Diversifying the modes of communication can keep the interaction exciting and dynamic. Video calls, voice messages, emails, and instant messaging should all be part of your communication toolkit. Each method has its own charm and utility, catering to different emotional and practical needs.

3. Engage in Shared Activities: Participating in activities together, even when apart, can significantly enhance

emotional closeness. This can include watching a movie simultaneously while on a video call, playing online games together, or even reading the same book at the same time. These shared experiences create common memories and topics for deeper conversations.

4. Be Open and Honest About Feelings: Transparency about one's feelings plays a critical role in deepening trust and understanding. "Honesty is the first chapter in the book of wisdom," Thomas Jefferson once remarked. Discuss your fears, joys, and daily struggles. This openness fosters a supportive environment where both partners feel secure to express their true selves.

5. Celebrate Important Occasions Together: Despite the distance, make an effort to celebrate birthdays, anniversaries, or professional achievements together. Whether it's a virtual date or sending a thoughtful gift, recognising and celebrating important milestones together strengthens the emotional bond.

6. Practice Active Listening: Effective communication isn't just about talking; it's equally about listening. Active listening involves paying full attention to your partner's words, asking clarifying questions, and responding thoughtfully. This practice assures your partner that their thoughts and feelings are valued and understood.

Incorporating these strategies into your communication routine can bridge the physical gap, ensuring that the emotional closeness in your relationship remains strong and resilient.

TIPS #3: Never reveal everything about yourself; keeping some things mysterious can make the relationship healthier.

Chapter 3

Making Time when There's None

Scheduling Regular Check-ins Despite Differing Time Zones

Scheduling regular check-ins despite differing time zones is a vital strategy for maintaining communication and emotional connection in long-distance relationships. Despite the challenges posed by geographical separation and varying schedules, consistent communication is key to nurturing the relationship. Here are some effective approaches to scheduling regular check-ins across different time zones:

1. Establish a Communication Schedule: Agree on specific times and days for regular check-ins that accommodate both partners' schedules as much as

possible. Flexibility is essential in finding time slots that work for both, considering factors such as work hours, personal commitments, and time zone differences.

2. Use Technology to Your Advantage: Leverage technology to facilitate communication despite time zone disparities. Set reminders on your phones or calendars for scheduled calls or video chats. Additionally, consider using world clock apps or websites to easily determine the best times for communication based on both partners' time zones.

3. Rotate Check-In Times: To ensure equitable participation and accommodate each other's schedules, rotate the timing of check-ins. Alternate between mornings, afternoons, and evenings to distribute the inconvenience of time zone differences more evenly.

4. Prioritise Quality Over Quantity: While regular check-ins are important, the quality of communication matters more than the frequency. Use the time you have together wisely, focusing on meaningful conversations and emotional connection. Quality interactions can help bridge the physical gap and strengthen the bond between partners.

5. Plan Ahead for Special Occasions: Be proactive in planning check-ins for special occasions such as birthdays, anniversaries, or holidays. Coordinate with your partner in advance to ensure that you both set aside time to celebrate and connect, despite the time zone challenges.

6. Be Understanding and Flexible: Recognise that maintaining communication across different time zones requires compromise and understanding from both partners. Be patient and flexible in accommodating each other's schedules and communicate openly about any challenges or conflicts that arise.

7. Embrace Asynchronous Communication: In addition to real-time check-ins, embrace asynchronous communication methods such as texting, emailing, or leaving voice messages. This allows you to stay connected and share updates even when synchronous communication is not feasible.

By implementing these strategies, couples in long-distance relationships can navigate time zone differences effectively, ensuring regular check-ins to sustain emotional closeness and strengthen their bond despite the miles apart.

TIPS #4 Even if you are busy, try to spend at least 30 minutes with him or her.

Balancing Relationship Needs With Personal and Professional Commitments

Balancing relationship needs with personal and professional commitments is a delicate dance, requiring intentionality and mindful planning. Here are some strategies, accompanied by insightful quotes, to help you maintain equilibrium in your life:

1. Prioritise Communication

"Communication in a relationship is like oxygen in life. Without it... it dies."

— *Tony Gaskins*

Schedule regular check-ins with your partner to discuss your respective commitments, priorities, and support needs. Transparency strengthens understanding and fosters a supportive environment.

2. Set Boundaries

"You can't pour from an empty cup. Take care of yourself first."

— *Eleanor Brownn*

Define clear boundaries between work, personal time, and relationship commitments. Respect these boundaries to prevent burnout and ensure that each aspect of your life receives the attention it deserves.

3. Practice Time Management.

> **"The key is not to prioritise what's on your schedule, but to schedule your priorities."**
>
> — *Stephen Covey*

Prioritise tasks based on urgency and importance, allocating dedicated time slots for work, self-care, and quality time with your partner. Utilise time management tools to stay organised and focused.

4. Schedule Regular Date Nights

> **"The best use of life is love. The best expression of love is time. The best time to love is now."**
>
> — *Rick Warren*

Make quality time with your partner non-negotiable by scheduling regular date nights or leisure activities.

These moments of intimacy strengthen your bond and nurture your relationship.

5. Be Flexible and Adapt

> ## *"Life is what happens when you're busy making other plans."*
>
> — *John Lennon*

Embrace flexibility in adjusting your schedules and expectations to accommodate unforeseen circumstances or changes in priorities. Approach challenges as a team, supporting each other through life's ups and downs.

6. Practice Self-Care

> ## *"Self-care is giving the world the best of you, instead of what's left of you."*
>
> — *Katie Reed*

Prioritise self-care activities that rejuvenate and recharge you, whether it's exercise, hobbies, or relaxation techniques. Taking care of yourself enables you to show up fully in your relationship and other areas of your life.

7. Seek Support When Needed.

> **"The best way to get through any challenge is to lean on each other."**
>
> *— Unknown*

Don't hesitate to seek support from your partner, friends, or family members when feeling overwhelmed. Share your concerns and collaborate on finding solutions that address both your individual and relationship needs.

By incorporating these strategies, accompanied by insightful quotes, you can navigate the complexities of balancing relationship needs with personal and professional commitments, fostering a harmonious and fulfilling life.

Tip #5: Prioritise Quality Time Together: Allocate dedicated time for meaningful interactions and shared activities with your partner. Quality time strengthens emotional bonds and fosters a deeper connection, laying the foundation for a healthy and fulfilling relationship.

Chapter 4

Emotional Intimacy from Afar

Building and Sustaining Emotional Intimacy Without Physical Presence

Building and sustaining emotional intimacy without physical presence is essential for maintaining a strong and fulfilling connection in long-distance relationships. Despite the miles between partners, there are several effective strategies to foster emotional closeness and deepen the bond. Here are some simple quotes and tips to guide you:

1. Prioritise Communication

> **"Distance means so little when someone means so much."**
>
> — *Unknown*

Make communication a priority by scheduling regular video calls, phone chats, or text messages. Share your thoughts, feelings, and experiences to stay connected on an emotional level.

2. Practice Active Listening.

> **"The most basic of all human needs is the need to understand and be understood."**
>
> — *Ralph Nichols*

Listen attentively to your partner's words, thoughts, and emotions. Validate their feelings and provide support without judgement, fostering trust and emotional intimacy.

3. Share Daily Life Moments.

> **"Happiness is only real when shared."**
>
> — *Jon Krakauer*

Share the little moments of your daily life, such as funny anecdotes, challenges, or achievements. These shared experiences create a sense of togetherness and strengthen the emotional bond.

4. Be Vulnerable and Honest.

> **"Authenticity is the daily practice of letting go of who we think we're supposed to be and embracing who we are."**
>
> — *Brené Brown*

Be open and honest about your thoughts, feelings, and vulnerabilities. Share your fears, insecurities, and dreams with your partner, allowing for a deeper emotional connection and understanding.

5. Plan Meaningful Virtual Dates.

> ***"Love knows no distance; it hath no continent."***
>
> *— William Penn*

Plan virtual dates or activities to create shared experiences despite physical distance. Watch movies together, play online games, or cook the same recipe while video calling each other.

6. Express Gratitude and Appreciation

> ***"Feeling gratitude and not expressing it is like wrapping a present and not giving it."***
>
> *— William Arthur Ward*

Regularly express gratitude and appreciation for your partner's presence, support, and love. Small gestures of appreciation go a long way in strengthening emotional intimacy.

7. Maintain Trust and Transparency.

"Trust is the glue of life. It's the most essential ingredient in effective communication. It's the foundational principle that holds all relationships."

— *Stephen Covey*

Build and maintain trust by being transparent and reliable in your communication. Honesty and integrity form the foundation of a strong and lasting emotional connection.

8. Protect Privacy and Security

"Never expose your travel pics on social media."

— *Unknown*

Safeguard your privacy and security by refraining from sharing personal or sensitive information, including travel photos, on social media. Maintain boundaries to protect your relationship and ensure intimacy remains between you and your partner.

By incorporating these quotes and strategies into your long-distance relationship, you can cultivate and sustain emotional intimacy, despite the physical distance separating you and your partner.

Creative Ideas for Sharing Experiences and Creating Memories Together

Creating shared experiences and memories together is essential for strengthening the bond and maintaining an emotional connection in long-distance relationships. Despite the physical distance, there are numerous creative ways to share moments and build lasting memories with your partner. Here are some inspirational quotes and practical suggestions to guide you:

1. Virtual Adventures

"Adventure is worthwhile in itself."

— *Amelia Earhart*

Plan virtual adventures, such as exploring online museums, taking virtual tours of landmarks, or watching live streams of wildlife. These experiences allow you to create shared memories and excitement from afar.

2. Cook Together

"The fondest memories are made gathered around the table."

— Unknown

Choose a recipe together and cook it simultaneously while video calling. Share laughs, culinary tips and the satisfaction of creating a delicious meal together, despite being in different locations.

3. Online Games and Challenges

"Life is more fun if you play games."

— Roald Dahl

Engage in online games or challenges, such as quizzes, multiplayer video games, or virtual escape rooms. These activities provide opportunities for friendly competition and shared laughter, fostering a sense of camaraderie.

4. Watch Movies or Shows Together

> *"Movies touch our hearts and awaken our vision."*
>
> — *Martin Scorsese*

Coordinate movie or TV show screenings by synchronising playback and using video chat to share reactions in real-time. Discuss your favourite scenes and characters afterwards, deepening your connection through shared interests.

5. Create Digital Scrapbooks

> *"Memories are timeless treasures of the heart."*
>
> — *Unknown*

Compile digital scrapbooks or photo albums of your shared experiences and milestones. Include photos, screenshots of conversations, and meaningful quotes to reminisce about your journey together.

6. Exchange Surprise Care Packages

"The greatest gift you can give someone is your time, your attention, your love, your concern."

— *Unknown*

Surprise your partner with thoughtful care packages containing handwritten letters, favourite snacks, or small gifts. These tangible expressions of love and affection create memorable moments of joy and connection.

7. Plan Future Adventures

"The best is yet to come."

— *Unknown*

Dream and plan future adventures together, whether it's travelling to new destinations, pursuing shared hobbies, or achieving personal goals. Visualising your future together strengthens your bond and creates anticipation for what lies ahead.

By incorporating these creative ideas into your long-distance relationship, you can share meaningful experiences and create lasting memories with your partner, despite the physical distance separating you.

TIPS #6: Choose activities that resonate with both you and your partner's interests and preferences to ensure that shared experiences are enjoyable and meaningful for both of you.

TIP #7: Capture his or her natural expressions in a picture to impress him or her.

Chapter 5

Trust and Transparency

The Importance of Trust in LDRs: How to Build and Sustain It

In long-distance relationships (LDRs), trust serves as the cornerstone that sustains the connection despite physical separation. Trust is not merely the absence of suspicion but the presence of confidence and reliability in your partner's words, actions, and intentions. Here are some insights, accompanied by quotes, on the importance of trust in LDRs and how to build and sustain it:

1. Foundation of Security

   Trust provides a sense of security and reassurance, allowing partners to feel emotionally safe and supported in their relationship. As Maya Angelou once said, "Have enough courage to trust love one more time and always one more time."

2. Building Trust Over Time

   Trust is not built overnight but is cultivated through consistent actions and behaviours over time. As Ralph Waldo Emerson remarked, "The glory of friendship is not the outstretched hand, not the kindly smile, nor the joy of companionship; it is the spiritual inspiration that comes to one when they discover that someone else believes in them and is willing to trust them."

3. Transparency and Vulnerability

   Transparency and vulnerability are essential components of trust in LDRs. It requires openness and honesty in sharing thoughts, feelings, and experiences with your partner. Brené Brown aptly stated, "Vulnerability is the birthplace of connection and the path to the feeling of worthiness. If it doesn't feel vulnerable, the sharing is probably not constructive."

4. Addressing Trust Issues

   Trust issues may arise due to past experiences or insecurities, but they can be overcome with patience, understanding, and effort from both partners. As Stephen Covey wisely advised, "Trust is the glue of life. It's the most essential ingredient in effective communication. It's the foundational principle that holds all relationships."

5. Honouring Commitments

Trust is reinforced through honouring commitments and promises made to each other. Actions speak louder than words, and consistent follow-through builds confidence and reliability in the relationship. As Lao Tzu famously said, "Watch your thoughts, they become your words; watch your words, they become your actions; watch your actions, they become your habits; watch your habits, they become your character; watch your character, it becomes your destiny."

By prioritising trust, transparency, and vulnerability in your long-distance relationship, you can build a strong foundation of connection and intimacy that withstands the challenges of physical separation. As you navigate the journey together, remember that trust is not a destination but a continuous journey of growth and mutual support.

TIPS#8 Prioritise open and honest communication with your partner, as transparency is key to building and sustaining trust in your long-distance relationship.

Understanding the Role of Past Experiences in Trust Issues

Understanding the role of past experiences in trust issues is crucial for fostering healing and growth in relationships. Past experiences, whether positive or negative, shape our perceptions, expectations, and behaviours in future relationships. Here's a closer look at this topic, accompanied by quotes:

1. Impact of Past Relationships

   Past relationships can leave lasting impressions on our psyche, influencing our trust levels and ability to open up to new partners. As Maya Angelou famously said, "I've learned that people will forget what you said, people will forget what you did, but people will never forget how you made them feel."

2. Childhood Experiences

   Childhood experiences, particularly those related to family dynamics and attachment styles, can significantly impact trust formation in adulthood. As John Bowlby, the father of attachment theory, noted, "Attachment theory is not formulated as a general theory of relationships; it addresses only a specific facet: the way in which human beings respond within relationships when hurt, separated from loved ones, or perceiving a threat."

3. Betrayal and Trauma

   Betrayal or trauma in past relationships can create deep-seated wounds that affect our ability to trust others. These experiences may lead to heightened vigilance, fear of vulnerability, or difficulty in forming intimate connections.

4. Learning from Past Mistakes

   While past experiences may have caused pain or mistrust, they also offer valuable lessons for growth and self-awareness. As Oprah Winfrey once said, "The greatest discovery of all time is that a person can change their future by merely changing their attitude."

5. Communicating with Your Partner

   Effective communication with your partner is essential for navigating trust issues stemming from past experiences. Be open and honest about your feelings, fears, and triggers, fostering understanding and empathy between you. As Harriet Lerner aptly said, "An apology is the super glue of life. It can repair just about anything."

By understanding the role of past experiences in trust issues, you can cultivate empathy, resilience and healing in your relationship, fostering a deeper sense of connection and trust with your partner.

TIPS #9: "Try to understand past bad experiences but never repeat them."

Setting Expectations and Establishing Trustworthiness

Setting expectations and establishing trustworthiness are fundamental aspects of building a strong foundation in any relationship, especially in long-distance ones. Here's a closer look at this topic, accompanied by quotes and insights:

1. Clarity in Expectations

   Setting clear and realistic expectations lays the groundwork for a healthy and fulfilling relationship. As Tony Robbins once said, "Setting goals is the first step in turning the invisible into the visible." Clearly communicate your needs, boundaries, and aspirations with your partner to ensure mutual understanding and alignment.

2. Consistency and Reliability

   Consistency and reliability are essential components of trustworthiness. Your actions should align with your words, demonstrating reliability and accountability over time. Maya Angelou famously remarked, "I've learned that people will forget what you said, people will forget what you did, but people will never forget how you made them feel." Consistently honour your commitments and follow-through on promises to earn your partner's trust.

3. Transparency and Openness

   Transparency and openness foster trust by creating a safe space for vulnerability and honesty. Be willing to share your thoughts, feelings, and experiences with your partner, even when it's uncomfortable. Brené Brown aptly stated, "Vulnerability is the birthplace of connection and the path to the feeling of worthiness. If it doesn't feel vulnerable, the sharing is probably not constructive." Embrace vulnerability as a means to deepen your connection and build trust.

4. Accountability and Ownership

   Take responsibility for your actions and their impact on your partner. If mistakes are made or trust is breached, own up to them and take steps to make amends. As Stephen Covey wisely advised, "Accountability breeds response-ability." By holding yourself accountable, you demonstrate integrity and respect for your partner's feelings.

5. Mutual Respect

   Respect forms the cornerstone of trustworthiness in any relationship. Treat your partner with kindness, empathy, and dignity, honouring their perspectives and boundaries. As H. Jackson Brown Jr. aptly said, "Let the refining and improving of your own life keep you so busy that you have little time to criticise others." Cultivate mutual respect by valuing and appreciating each other's unique qualities and contributions.

By setting clear expectations, demonstrating consistency and reliability, fostering transparency and openness, embracing accountability, and prioritising mutual respect, you can establish trustworthiness and strengthen the foundation of your long-distance relationship. Remember, trust is built through consistent actions and genuine efforts to uphold integrity and honour your partner's trust.

TIPS#10 **"Never do things to others that you wouldn't want them to do to you."**

The Impact of Honesty and Transparency on Relationship Dynamics

Honesty and transparency play pivotal roles in shaping the dynamics of any relationship, including long-distance ones. Here's an exploration of their impact, accompanied by quotes and insights:

1. Foundation of Trust

   Honesty and transparency form the bedrock of trust in a relationship. When partners are open and truthful with each other, they foster a sense of security and reliability. As Oprah Winfrey famously stated, "The truth is, unless you let go, unless you forgive yourself, unless you forgive the situation, unless you realise that the situation is over, you cannot move forward."

2. Fostering Intimacy

    Honest and transparent communication fosters deeper emotional intimacy between partners. By sharing their thoughts, feelings, and vulnerabilities openly, couples create a safe space for authentic connection. Brené Brown aptly noted, "Vulnerability is the birthplace of love, belonging, joy, courage, empathy, and creativity. It is the source of hope, empathy, accountability, and authenticity."

3. Resolving Conflict

    Honesty and transparency are essential for effectively resolving conflicts in a relationship. When partners communicate openly and honestly about their concerns and feelings, they can address misunderstandings and work towards solutions together. As John C. Maxwell wisely said, "Honesty and transparency make you vulnerable. Be honest and transparent anyway."

4. Building Mutual Respect

    Honest and transparent communication cultivates mutual respect between partners. By valuing each other's perspectives and being truthful in their interactions, couples demonstrate respect for each other's feelings and opinions. As Mandy Hale aptly put it, "Respect yourself enough to walk away from anything that no longer serves you, grows you, or makes you happy."

5. Strengthening Commitment

Honesty and transparency reinforce commitment in a relationship by creating a strong foundation of trust and authenticity. When partners are truthful and open with each other, they deepen their emotional connection and strengthen their resolve to overcome challenges together. As Maya Angelou once said, "When someone shows you who they are, believe them the first time."

By prioritising honesty and transparency in your long-distance relationship, you can foster trust, intimacy, respect, and commitment, laying the groundwork for a strong and fulfilling partnership. Remember, open communication and authenticity are essential ingredients for navigating the challenges of distance and building a lasting connection with your partner.

TIPS#11: "Always be honest in your relationship, as one partner will always look better than the other, and there are no limits to this."

Recognising and Addressing Red Flags in Trust Issues

Recognising and addressing red flags in trust issues is vital for maintaining a healthy and fulfilling long-distance relationship. Here's an exploration of this topic, accompanied by quotes:

1. Awareness of Red Flags

    It's crucial to be aware of potential red flags that may indicate trust issues in your relationship. These could include inconsistencies in your partner's stories, secretive behaviour, or a lack of transparency in communication. As Maya Angelou wisely said, "When someone shows you who they are, believe them the first time."

2. Open Communication

    Open and honest communication is key to addressing red flags in trust issues. Express your concerns and observations to your partner in a non-confrontational manner, encouraging them to share their perspective. Brené Brown aptly noted, "Clear is kind. Unclear is unkind."

3. Addressing Past Trauma

    Past traumas or negative experiences can contribute to trust issues in a relationship. It's essential to acknowledge and address any unresolved trauma that may be impacting your ability to trust or be trusted. As Oprah Winfrey wisely said, "You have to acknowledge your truth and not let anyone else define your life. And the only way you can do that is by digging deep and figuring out who you truly are."

4. Establishing Boundaries

   Clear boundaries are essential for rebuilding trust and creating a sense of safety in your relationship. Clearly define your expectations and boundaries with your partner, and respect each other's limits. As Anne Katherine aptly said, "Boundaries are a part of self-care. They are healthy, normal, and necessary."

5. Commitment to Growth

   Both partners must be committed to addressing trust issues and working towards growth and healing together. It requires patience, understanding, and a willingness to confront uncomfortable truths. As John C. Maxwell wisely advised, "The greatest mistake we make is living in constant fear that we will make one."

By recognising and addressing red flags in trust issues with open communication, addressing past trauma, establishing boundaries, and committing to growth together, you can navigate challenges and build a stronger, more trusting long-distance relationship. Remember, trust is a journey that requires effort, understanding, and a shared commitment to building a healthy and fulfilling partnership.

TIPS #12: "Never react to everything; instead, respond. Sometimes, they may express anger when they feel lonely, so it's important to stay calm."

Handling Jealousy and Insecurity in the Absence of Physical Proximity

Handling jealousy and insecurity in the absence of physical proximity is a common challenge faced by many in long-distance relationships. Here's a detailed exploration of this topic, accompanied by quotes:

1. Understanding Triggers

    Jealousy and insecurity often stem from underlying fears and insecurities. It's essential to identify the specific triggers that evoke these emotions, whether it's fear of abandonment, past experiences, or lack of clarity. As Susan Winter aptly stated, "Jealousy isn't a sign of love; it's a sign of insecurity."

2. Building Trust

    Building trust is key to overcoming jealousy and insecurity. Trust is earned through consistent actions and behaviours over time. Both partners must demonstrate reliability, honesty, and transparency to cultivate trust in the relationship. As Ernest Hemingway aptly said, "The best way to find out if you can trust somebody is to trust them."

3. Setting Boundaries

    Setting clear boundaries helps manage jealousy and insecurity by providing a sense of security and predictability. Establish boundaries regarding communication with others, social media usage, and personal space to alleviate feelings of jealousy and insecurity. As Anne Katherine wisely advised, "Boundaries are a part of self-care. They are healthy, normal, and necessary."

4. Self-Reflection and Self-Care

Take time for self-reflection and self-care to address underlying insecurities and build resilience. Practice self-compassion and self-love, acknowledging your worth independent of the relationship. Engage in activities that bring you joy and fulfilment, nurturing your emotional well-being. As Lucille Ball aptly stated, "Love yourself first, and everything else falls into line."

Handling jealousy and insecurity in a long-distance relationship requires patience, understanding, and a commitment to building trust, setting boundaries, and prioritising self-care. By addressing underlying triggers, fostering trust, setting boundaries, and prioritising self-care, you can navigate these challenges and cultivate a healthy and fulfilling relationship, despite the physical distance. Remember, overcoming jealousy and insecurity is a journey that requires effort and mutual support from both partners.

TIPS #13: "Never share your relationship issues with anyone because a third person may not know your partner better than you do, which can exacerbate the issue."

Chapter 6

The Financial Aspect of Love

Budgeting for Travel and Managing Financial Constraints

Budgeting for travel and managing financial constraints is essential for individuals in long-distance relationships who often incur expenses related to visits and maintaining communication. Here's a detailed exploration of this topic, accompanied by quotes:

1. Establishing a Travel Fund

   Create a dedicated travel fund specifically allocated for visits to see your partner or for them to come see you. Set aside a portion of your income each month towards this fund to ensure you have the financial resources available when needed. As Dave Ramsey aptly stated, "A budget is telling your money where to go instead of wondering where it went."

2. Prioritising Essential Expenses

    Identify essential expenses in your budget and prioritise them over discretionary spending. Cut back on non-essential purchases to allocate more funds towards travel and communication expenses related to your long-distance relationship. As Suze Orman wisely advised, "Look at your budget realistically and make sure that you're spending less than you earn."

3. Researching Cost-Saving Strategies

    Explore cost-saving strategies such as booking flights and accommodations in advance, taking advantage of travel rewards programmes, and opting for budget-friendly transportation options. Additionally, consider visiting your partner during off-peak travel seasons to save on expenses. As Arthur Frommer aptly stated, "The best way to save money on travel is to travel off-season."

4. Communicating Financial Boundaries

    Have open and honest discussions with your partner about financial constraints and set realistic expectations regarding visits and shared expenses. Transparency and understanding are crucial for navigating financial challenges in a long-distance relationship. As Oprah Winfrey wisely said,

"The more you praise and celebrate your life, the more there is in life to celebrate."

5. Exploring Alternative Communication Methods

In addition to in-person visits, explore alternative communication methods such as video calls, voice messages, and handwritten letters as cost-effective ways to stay connected with your partner. These methods can help bridge the distance between visits while minimising expenses. As Mother Teresa aptly stated, "Spread love everywhere you go. Let no one ever come to you without leaving happier."

By establishing a travel fund, prioritising essential expenses, researching cost-saving strategies, communicating financial boundaries, and exploring alternative communication methods, individuals in long-distance relationships can effectively manage financial constraints while nurturing their connection. Remember, with careful planning and communication, it's possible to maintain a fulfilling relationship without breaking the bank.

TIPS #14: "Travelling and spending time together can help bridge the gap and create lasting memories."

Planning for Financially Sustainable Ways to Maintain the Relationship

Planning for financially sustainable ways to maintain a long-distance relationship is crucial for ensuring that both partners can comfortably sustain the connection without undue financial strain. Here's a detailed exploration of this topic, accompanied by quotes:

1. Establishing Financial Goals

    Start by discussing your financial goals as a couple and creating a budget that aligns with your priorities. Set clear objectives for how much you can comfortably afford to allocate towards visits, communication expenses, and other relationship-related costs. As Warren Buffett aptly stated, "Do not save what is left after spending, but spend what is left after saving."

2. Maximising Cost-Effective Communication

    Utilise cost-effective communication methods such as video calls, voice messages, and texting to stay connected with your partner without breaking the bank. Take advantage of free or low-cost communication apps and platforms to minimise expenses while maintaining regular contact. As H. Jackson Brown Jr. wisely advised, "Live so that when your children think of fairness, caring, and integrity, they think of you."

3. Planning Visits Wisely

    Plan visits strategically to make the most of your travel budget. Look for deals on flights, accommodations, and transportation options to minimise costs. Consider alternating visits between partners' locations to share the financial burden evenly. As Arthur Frommer aptly stated, "The more you praise and celebrate your life, the more there is in life to celebrate."

4. Exploring Shared Experiences

    Explore shared experiences that don't require a significant financial investment, such as cooking together virtually, watching movies simultaneously, or participating in online activities and games. These activities can help strengthen your bond without adding financial strain. As Maya Angelou aptly said, "I sustain myself with the love of family."

5. Saving for Future Milestones

    Set aside savings for future milestones in your relationship, such as moving in together or getting married. By planning and saving strategically, you can ensure that you're financially prepared for significant transitions in your relationship. As Dave Ramsey wisely advised, "Financial peace isn't the acquisition of stuff. It's learning to live on less than you make, so you can give money back and have money to invest."

By establishing financial goals, maximising cost-effective communication, planning visits wisely, exploring shared experiences, and saving for future milestones, you can maintain a financially sustainable long-distance relationship while nurturing your connection. Remember, open communication and mutual understanding are essential for navigating financial challenges and building a strong foundation for your relationship.

TIPS #15: "Improving your financial status can help both of you grow together and obtain financial freedom."

Chapter 7

Making the Most of Visits: Do's and Don'ts

Guidelines for Maximising Enjoyment and Strengthening Bonds During Visits

Maximising enjoyment and strengthening bonds during visits in a long-distance relationship requires thoughtful planning and intentional actions. Here are some guidelines to help you make the most of your time together:

1. Plan Meaningful Activities:

    Schedule activities that allow you to connect on a deeper level and create lasting memories. Consider exploring new places, engaging in shared hobbies, or simply spending quality time together in meaningful conversations.

2. Communicate Openly:

   Foster open and honest communication throughout the visit. Share your thoughts, feelings, and experiences with each other, and actively listen to your partner's perspective. Effective communication strengthens emotional bonds and promotes understanding.

3. Be Present:

   Focus on being fully present and engaged in the moment with your partner. Minimise distractions such as phones or work-related matters and devote your attention to each other. Embrace the opportunity to connect on a deeper level without external interruptions.

4. Show Affection:

   Express your love and affection towards your partner through physical gestures, verbal affirmations, and acts of kindness. Small gestures of affection, such as holding hands or giving compliments, can go a long way in strengthening your bond and fostering intimacy.

5. Create Shared Experiences:

   Engage in activities that allow you to create shared experiences and build a sense of togetherness. Whether it's cooking a meal together, going for a hike, or attending a local event, shared experiences strengthen your connection and create lasting memories.

6. Practice Gratitude:

Express gratitude for the time spent together and the opportunity to strengthen your relationship. Acknowledge and appreciate the efforts made by both partners to maintain the connection despite the distance. Gratitude fosters positivity and deepens emotional bonds.

7. Be Flexible and Spontaneous:

While it's important to have a general plan for the visit, leave room for spontaneity and flexibility. Embrace unexpected opportunities and be open to trying new things together. Spontaneous adventures often lead to some of the most memorable experiences.

By following these guidelines, you can maximise enjoyment and strengthen the bonds with your partner during visits in your long-distance relationship. Remember, the key is to prioritise quality time, open communication, and shared experiences to create meaningful connections that endure beyond the visit.

TIPS #15 Whenever you meet your partner or leave them, hug them softly and kiss their forehead.

Don'ts

1. Avoid Conflict: Refrain from engaging in unnecessary arguments or conflicts during the visit. Practice patience, understanding, and compromise to resolve disagreements amicably.

2. Limit Distractions: Minimise distractions such as phones, laptops, or other electronic devices that may detract from quality time spent together. Focus on being fully present and engaged in each other's company.

3. Over plan: While it's important to have a general itinerary, avoid overplanning every minute of the visit. Leave room for spontaneity and flexibility to enjoy unexpected opportunities and experiences.

4. Neglect Self-Care: Don't neglect your own well-being during the visit. Prioritise self-care activities such as rest, relaxation, and nourishing meals to ensure you're physically and emotionally rejuvenated.

5. Rush Goodbyes: Avoid rushing goodbyes at the end of the visit. Take the time to say goodbye properly, express gratitude for the time spent together, and reaffirm your commitment to each other.

TIP #16: Never check your partner's phone or messages when they are not around.

Managing Emotions and Coping Strategies for the Post-departure Period

Managing emotions and coping strategies for the post-departure period in a long-distance relationship are essential for maintaining emotional well-being and navigating the challenges of separation. Here's a detailed exploration of this topic:

1. Allow Yourself to Feel:

    It's normal to experience a range of emotions after parting ways with your partner. Allow yourself to feel whatever emotions arise, whether it's sadness, loneliness, or longing. Recognise that these feelings are valid and part of the natural process of adjusting to being apart.

2. Stay Connected:

    Maintain regular communication with your partner through calls, texts, or video chats to stay connected despite the distance. Sharing your thoughts and emotions with each other can provide comfort and support during difficult times. Knowing that your partner is there for you can alleviate feelings of loneliness and isolation.

3. Engage in Self-Care:

    Prioritise self-care activities to nurture your physical, emotional, and mental well-being. Practise activities that help you relax and unwind, such as exercising, meditating, or indulging in hobbies you enjoy. Taking care of yourself empowers you to cope with the challenges of separation more effectively.

4. Focus on the Positive:

    Shift your focus towards the positive aspects of your relationship and the experiences you shared during your time together. Remind yourself of the love, connection, and support you have with your partner, even when physically apart. Cultivating a positive mindset can help counteract feelings of sadness and despair.

5. Establish a Routine:

    Establishing a daily routine can provide structure and stability during the post-departure period. Plan activities and tasks that give you a sense of purpose and accomplishment, whether it's work, hobbies, or spending time with friends and family. A structured routine can help distract you from feelings of emptiness and facilitate a smoother transition.

6. Lean on Support Systems:

    Seek support from friends, family members, or online communities who understand what you're going through. Sharing your feelings and experiences with others who empathise can provide validation and comfort. Surround yourself with people who uplift and support you during challenging times.

7. Practice Mindfulness:

Incorporate mindfulness techniques into your daily life to cultivate awareness and acceptance of your emotions. Practice mindfulness meditation, deep breathing exercises, or grounding techniques to stay present and manage stress and anxiety effectively.

By implementing these coping strategies, you can navigate the post-departure period in your long-distance relationship with resilience and emotional strength. Remember, it's okay to seek support and take care of yourself during this time of transition. With time and practice, you'll develop healthy ways to manage your emotions and maintain a strong connection with your partner, despite the distance.

Chapter 8

The Long Haul: Maintaining Long-Term Goals

Setting Mutual Goals and Future Plans As a Couple

Setting mutual goals and future plans as a couple in a long-distance relationship is crucial for fostering a sense of unity, purpose, and a shared vision. Here's a detailed exploration of this topic, accompanied by quotes and the idea of a vision board:

1. Establishing Shared Aspirations:

> **"The future belongs to those
> who believe in the beauty of
> their dreams."**
>
> *— Eleanor Roosevelt*

Begin by discussing your individual aspirations, dreams, and ambitions with your partner. Identify common interests, values, and goals that you both share and align with. This process allows you to create a foundation for setting mutual goals and future plans together.

2. Defining Short-Term and Long-Term Objectives:

> **"A goal without a plan is just
> a wish."**
>
> *— Antoine de Saint-Exupéry*

Outline both short-term and long-term objectives that you want to achieve as a couple. Short-term goals may include planning visits, improving communication, or working towards personal development. Long-term goals may involve milestones such as moving in together, pursuing education or career advancement, or starting a family.

3. Prioritising Communication and Collaboration:

"Communication in a relationship is like oxygen to life. Without it... it dies."

— *Tony Gaskins*

Maintain open and transparent communication throughout the goal-setting process. Listen actively to your partner's desires, concerns, and ideas, and collaborate on finding common ground. Respect each other's perspectives and work together as a team to develop achievable goals.

4. Creating SMART Goals:

"Setting goals is the first step in turning the invisible into the visible."

— *Tony Robbins.*

Ensure that your goals are Specific, Measurable, Achievable, Relevant, and Time-bound (SMART). Break down larger goals into smaller, actionable steps that you can work towards incrementally. This approach helps you track progress, stay motivated, and celebrate achievements along the way.

5. Adapting to Change and Flexibility:

> **"The measure of intelligence is the ability to change."**
>
> — *Albert Einstein.*

Remain flexible and adaptable as circumstances may change over time. Be prepared to adjust your goals and plans accordingly to accommodate new opportunities or challenges that arise. Embrace change as an opportunity for growth and learning, and maintain a positive attitude towards overcoming obstacles together.

6. Celebrating Milestones and Progress:

> **"In the end, it's not the years in your life that count. It's the life in your years."**
>
> — *Abraham Lincoln*

Celebrate your achievements and milestones as you progress towards your mutual goals. Acknowledge the hard work, dedication, and commitment you've both invested in your relationship and future plans. Celebrating successes strengthens your bond and motivates you to continue working towards your shared vision.

7. Revisiting and Revising Goals:

"Success is not final, failure is not fatal: It is the courage to continue that counts."

— Winston Churchill.

Periodically revisit and revise your goals as your relationship evolves and matures. Reflect on your progress, reassess your priorities, and realign your goals with your changing circumstances and aspirations. This ongoing process ensures that your goals remain relevant and meaningful to both partners.

Additionally, creating a vision board together can serve as a visual representation of your shared aspirations, dreams, and goals. Include images, quotes, and symbols that represent your collective vision for the future. Display the vision board in a prominent place where you can both see it regularly, serving as a constant reminder of the future you are building together.

TIPS#17 Never let your guard down for anyone; be a protector and stand with them.

Strategies for Growth and Enrichment in the Relationship Despite the Distance

Certainly, integrating financial planning, including mutual funds, side hustles, and investments, into your long-distance relationship can provide stability, growth, and shared goals. Here's how you can incorporate these elements:

1. Mutual Funds for Long-Term Financial Goals:

   Consider investing in mutual funds together to work towards long-term financial objectives, such as buying a house, travelling the world, or saving for retirement. Research different mutual fund options, assess your risk tolerance, and set up joint accounts to pool your resources and achieve your shared financial aspirations.

2. Side Hustles for Additional Income Streams:

   Explore opportunities for side hustles or part-time ventures that you can pursue together or individually. Whether it's freelancing, starting an online business, or monetising a hobby, side hustles can generate additional income streams to supplement your finances and fund your shared goals.

3. Investments for Wealth Accumulation:

   Diversify your investment portfolio by exploring various investment options, such as stocks, bonds, real estate, or cryptocurrencies. Educate yourself about investment strategies, assess your financial goals and risk tolerance, and collaborate on building a well-rounded investment portfolio that aligns with your long-term objectives.

4. Financial Planning and Budgeting:

   Develop a comprehensive financial plan and budget that outlines your income, expenses, savings, and investment goals. Allocate funds towards essential expenses, savings, debt repayment, and discretionary spending, and track your progress regularly to ensure you're staying on track towards your financial objectives.

5. Open Communication about Finances:

   Foster open and transparent communication about finances, including income, expenses, debts, and financial goals. Discuss your individual financial situations, values, and priorities, and work together to create a shared vision for your financial future.

6. Set Financial Milestones:

   Establish specific financial milestones that you want to achieve together, such as paying off debt, reaching a certain level of savings, or achieving a targeted rate of return on investments. Break down these milestones into achievable steps and celebrate your progress along the way.

7. Educate Yourselves about Personal Finance:

   Take the time to educate yourselves about personal finance, investment principles, and wealth-building strategies. Attend seminars, read books, or enrol in online courses together to deepen your understanding of financial concepts and empower yourselves to make informed financial decisions.

8. Support Each Other's Financial Goals:

   Respect each other's financial goals, values, and spending habits, and offer support and encouragement as you work towards your individual and shared objectives. Collaborate on financial decisions, compromise when necessary, and celebrate each other's financial achievements.

9. Monitor and Review Your Financial Plan:

   Regularly monitor and review your financial plan to track your progress, identify areas for improvement, and adjust your strategies as needed. Schedule periodic check-ins to discuss your financial situation, reassess your goals, and make any necessary course corrections.

10. Plan for the Future Together:

    Keep your long-term financial future in mind as you plan your life together. Discuss important financial milestones, such as buying a home, starting a family, or retiring early, and create a roadmap to achieve these goals together.

By integrating financial planning, including mutual funds, side hustles, and investments, into your long-distance relationship, you can build a solid foundation for financial stability, growth, and prosperity. Remember, open communication, mutual support, and shared goals are key to achieving financial success as a couple.

TIPS #18: Be open about financial transactions and plan for the future together.

Chapter 9

When Distance Ends: Transitioning to Proximity

Preparing for the End of the Distance: Think About Marriage

Preparing for the end of the distance inevitably involves considering marriage, which often entails seeking approval from families and preparing for married life together. Here are insights into these crucial aspects, accompanied by relevant quotes:

1. Family Approval:

> **"A successful marriage requires falling in love many times, always with the same person."**
>
> — *Mignon McLaughlin.*

Securing the approval of both families can be significant in many cultures and traditions. Before proceeding with marriage plans, ensure that both parents and families are supportive of your relationship and forthcoming marriage. Open communication, transparency, and patience are key when addressing any concerns or reservations they may have.

2. Building Relationships with In-Laws:

> **"Family is not an important thing. It's everything."**
>
> — *Michael J. Fox.*

Cultivating positive relationships with your future in-laws is essential for a harmonious married life. Take the time to get to know each other, show genuine interest and respect, and strive to establish a bond based on mutual understanding and acceptance.

3. Addressing Cultural Differences:

> *"Cultural differences should not separate us from each other, but rather cultural diversity brings a collective strength that can benefit all of humanity."*
>
> — Robert Alan

If you and your partner come from different cultural backgrounds, navigate potential cultural differences with sensitivity and respect. Discuss how you will incorporate each other's cultural traditions and values into your married life, ensuring that both partners feel understood and respected.

4. Marriage Life Expectations:

> **"Love does not consist of gazing at each other, but in looking outward together in the same direction."**
>
> — *Antoine de Saint-Exupéry*

Have candid discussions about your expectations for married life, including roles, responsibilities, and shared goals. Talk about important topics such as finances, career aspirations, family planning, and division of household chores. Understanding each other's expectations can help lay a solid foundation for a fulfilling marriage.

5. Conflict Resolution Skills:

> **"In every marriage, more than a week old, there are grounds for divorce. The trick is to find, and continue to find, grounds for marriage."**
>
> — *Robert Anderson.*

Strengthen your conflict resolution skills to navigate challenges and disagreements that may arise in married life. Practice active listening, empathy, and compromise, and develop effective communication strategies to resolve conflicts constructively and maintain harmony in your relationship.

TIPS#19 A successful relationship ends with a successful journey together.

Adjusting to Life Together After Living Apart

Adjusting to life together after living apart can indeed be challenging, even for celebrities who seemingly have it all. Let's take a look at a real-life example of a celebrity couple navigating this transition:

Consider the story of John Legend and Chrissy Teigen. Despite being deeply in love, their relationship began with geographical challenges. John, a Grammy-winning musician, and Chrissy, a model and television personality, initially maintained a long-distance relationship due to their demanding careers. They spent significant periods apart, with John travelling the world for tours and performances while Chrissy pursued her modelling and television projects.

However, despite the distance, their bond grew stronger over time. They communicated regularly, supported each other's careers, and cherished the time they spent together whenever their schedules allowed. Their love story captured the hearts of many as they openly shared their journey, including the challenges of living apart in the public eye.

As their relationship progressed, John and Chrissy made the decision to take the next step and move in together. Adjusting to life under the same roof presented its own set of challenges. They had to navigate merging their lifestyles, routines, and personal space while still maintaining their individual identities and careers.

"Love is friendship that has caught fire. It is quiet understanding, mutual confidence, sharing, and forgiving. It is loyalty through good and bad times. It settles for less than perfection and makes allowances for human weaknesses."

— Ann Landers.

Like any couple, John and Chrissy faced obstacles along the way. They had disagreements, moments of frustration, and adjustments to make. However, their commitment to each other and their willingness to communicate openly and honestly helped them overcome these challenges.

> **"Love is not about how many days, months or years you have been together. Love is about how much you love each other every single day."**
>
> — *Unknown*

Today, John Legend and Chrissy Teigen are not only happily married but also proud parents to two beautiful children. Their journey from a long-distance relationship to a harmonious life together serves as an inspiring example of love, resilience, and the power of communication in navigating the transition from living apart to sharing a life under the same roof.

> **"The best love is the kind that awakens the soul and makes us reach for more, that plants a fire in our hearts and brings peace to our minds."**
>
> — *Nicholas Sparks.*

Their story reminds us that even in the glamorous world of celebrities, adjusting to life together after living apart requires patience, understanding and a willingness to work through challenges as a team. With love, determination and mutual support, any couple can successfully transition from separate lives to a shared future filled with happiness and fulfilment.

TIPS#20 Two different people are together to understand each other.

Chapter 10

Stories from the Distance

Lessons Learned and Advice from Successful Long-distance Partnerships

Successful long-distance partnerships offer valuable lessons and advice for couples navigating the challenges of maintaining love and connection across distance. Here are some key insights gleaned from their experiences:

1. Prioritise Communication:

   Effective communication is the cornerstone of any successful long-distance relationship. Couples in thriving partnerships make time to connect regularly, whether through texts, calls, video chats, or handwritten letters. They prioritise honest and open communication, sharing their thoughts, feelings, and experiences to bridge the physical gap between them.

2. Cultivate Trust and Security:

    Trust is essential for the health of any relationship, but it becomes even more crucial in a long-distance partnership. Successful couples actively cultivate trust by being reliable, transparent, and consistent in their words and actions. They reassure each other of their commitment, address insecurities openly, and prioritise building a strong foundation of trust and security.

3. Embrace Independence and Growth:

    Thriving long-distance partnerships recognise the importance of individual growth and independence. Instead of viewing distance as a hindrance, couples see it as an opportunity for personal development and exploration. They support each other's goals and aspirations, encouraging independence while fostering a strong sense of partnership.

4. Plan Meaningful Visits and Shared Experiences:

    Visits play a crucial role in maintaining intimacy and connection in long-distance relationships. Successful couples prioritise planning meaningful visits and shared experiences to create lasting memories together. Whether exploring new places, enjoying quality time at home, or participating in activities they both love, these moments strengthen their bond and sustain their connection.

5. Practice Patience and Resilience:

Long-distance relationships require patience and resilience to navigate the challenges of distance and time apart. Successful couples understand that obstacles will arise, but they approach them with patience, adaptability and a positive mindset. They remain committed to overcoming challenges together, knowing that their love and bond are worth the effort.

6. Find Creative Ways to Stay Connected:

Distance may physically separate couples, but it doesn't have to diminish their connection. Successful partnerships find creative ways to stay connected and engaged in each other's lives, whether through virtual dates, surprise gifts, shared playlists, or collaborative projects. They prioritise finding innovative ways to nurture their connection despite the miles between them.

7. Celebrate Milestones and Achievements:

Every milestone, no matter how small, is an opportunity to celebrate the strength and resilience of the relationship. Successful couples acknowledge and celebrate each other's achievements, anniversaries, and special moments, reinforcing their bond and commitment to each other.

8. Foster Mutual Support and Understanding:

    Thriving long-distance partnerships are built on a foundation of mutual support and understanding. Couples actively listen to each other's needs, offer encouragement, and provide emotional support during both the highs and lows of life. They prioritise being each other's biggest cheerleaders, knowing that their unwavering support strengthens their connection.

9. Maintain a Positive Outlook:

    A positive outlook can make all the difference in maintaining a healthy and fulfilling long-distance relationship. Successful couples focus on the positives, appreciate the opportunities that distance brings, and remain optimistic about their future together. They approach challenges with resilience and determination, knowing that their love can conquer any obstacle.

10. Keep the End Goal in Sight:

    Perhaps most importantly, successful long-distance partnerships keep the end goal in sight. Whether it's closing the distance, starting a life together, or simply being reunited, couples maintain a shared vision for their future. They remain committed to their relationship, knowing that the challenges of distance are temporary and that their love will ultimately bring them together.

In conclusion, long-distance relationships are a testament to the power of love, resilience, and commitment. Despite the challenges of physical separation, couples who embark on this journey often discover newfound strengths within themselves and their relationships. Through effective communication, trust, independence, and unwavering support, they navigate the distance with grace and determination.

As this book has illustrated, successful long-distance partnerships are not without their trials, but they are also filled with moments of joy, growth, and profound connection. From prioritising communication and trust to embracing independence and celebrating shared experiences, couples can forge deep and meaningful connections that transcend physical distance.

Ultimately, the lessons learned and advice shared by couples in successful long-distance relationships serve as a beacon of hope for those embarking on similar journeys. They remind us that love knows no bounds and that, with patience, resilience, and unwavering commitment, even the greatest distances can be overcome.

Whether you are currently navigating a long-distance relationship, contemplating embarking on one, or simply seeking insight into the dynamics of love and connection, may the stories, advice, and wisdom shared in this book inspire and guide you on your journey.

Remember, distance may test the strength of a relationship, but it also has the power to deepen the bonds of love and appreciation. As you embark on your own journey of love across miles, may you find solace in the knowledge that true love knows no distance and that every obstacle you overcome brings you one step closer to the fulfilling and lasting connection you seek.

Here's to love that transcends boundaries, defies distance, and endures through every trial and triumph. May your journey be filled with love, laughter, and endless moments of shared joy, wherever in the world it may take you.